GW01607307

Published by G. Whizzard Publications Ltd.,
in association with André Deutsch Ltd.,
105 Great Russell Street, London W.C.1.

ISBN 233 96991 8

Printed in Italy by New Interlitho (SPA).

Filmsetting by Baird Harris Filmsetting Ltd., London.

 G. Whizzard/André Deutsch 

John Seymour's Gardening Book

Illustrated by Jonathon Coudrille

John Seymour's Gardening Book.

A gardening book for children by the author of **The Fat of the Land, Self-Sufficiency** and **The Complete Book of Self-Sufficiency.**

John Seymour's message is clear: growing your own vegetables is not only good for you and your family, it is also great fun to do. The book describes how even the smallest garden can be made highly productive with the right crops; it explains how to prepare the different kinds of soil, what effect the seasons have on the garden, and how to plan your planting so that something is coming up all year round. There are detailed growing instructions for all the better-known vegetables and herbs, as well as for one or two unusual ones. Finally, there are some general gardening tips and a comprehensive guide to selecting the right tools for the job.

CONTENTS

Introduction

There are few things in the world more fun than producing your own food, or the food to help feed your family. To take a piece of land which is all weeds and rubbish, dig it, cultivate it, sow seeds in it and see them grow into big beautiful plants, to look after them, and then, when they are quite ready, pick them and eat them, is a very satisfying and exciting thing to do.

The idea of this book is to show that it is not only grown-ups that can make gardens, or grow food; children can do it, too. There is no crop that your father or mother, your aunt or your uncle, can grow that you cannot grow just as well – if not better. And you don't need to live in the country or have a large garden to do it. Any small patch of ground will do, as long as you treat the soil properly and plant the right things.

One thing that some grown-ups have more of than some children is patience. And of course gardening does take patience; it's not like flying a kite or riding a skateboard, where you get your fun immediately you do it. You dig the ground and plant the seed – and then you have got to **wait**. True, with some crops like radishes or mustard-and-cress you don't have to wait long, but with others you do. Maybe even months.

But there is always something interesting going on in a garden. You can plant different things at different times, so that crops are coming up (and can be harvested) all the year round. The changing weather and seasons add to the fun. Once you start, you will find yourself rushing to the window first thing in the morning to see if it's raining to water your beans, or warm and dry for digging your potatoes, or a hard frost to nip off and damage your early peas. Nothing is certain about gardening, which makes everything a bit of a gamble.

Apart from the sheer enjoyment, it's really very rewarding to know that you are seriously contributing to the business of feeding your whole family. Vegetables bought in a shop are often many days old before they reach you and have lost all their freshness and delicacy of taste. Most of them have been produced on big farms where they are forced to grow extra fast and large by heavy doses of chemical fertilizers. This may increase their size, but it makes them tasteless. They will also have been poisoned with lots of other chemicals, used to destroy weeds and various insects, fungi and bacterial pests.

The vegetables you grow will be fresh, free of harmful chemicals, and full of flavour – and will do everyone who eats them lots of good.

As for the difficulty of gardening, well, very few things that are worthwhile and satisfying are easy. To grow good crops you have to know what you are doing and do it properly. A lot of this knowledge will come with experience, but if you read this book and take notice of what it says, you'll get off to a good start.

So, dig in – and happy gardening!

John Seymour

How do Plants Grow?

A plant has to have its roots in the ground, and the kind of ground that suits it. Some plants like light soil (soil with sand in it), some like heavy soil (soil with clay in it), some like loose soil, some firm, some need a lot of water in the soil, some much less, some like acid soil, some like soil with a lot of lime in it. But broadly speaking, all plants need soil to hold them up, and to feed them.

Plants eat by taking water into their roots, and with the water certain nutritious substances which are dissolved in it. The water, with these nutrients, or foods, in it, travels up the roots and the stem to the leaves. The sun shines on the leaves, and sunshine, being made of hot rays, is **energy.**

Now plants have got to have energy to live and grow, just as we have. Inside them is a green substance (it's actually what makes them green) called chlorophyll. This seizes the energy from the rays of the sun and uses it to change certain of the inorganic, or dead, foods that have been brought up from the ground by the water, together with certain chemicals taken from the air, into organic, or live, material.

This material is simply stored energy, which is carried around the plant by the water inside it. It's what makes the plant grow and take shape; it produces its seed and its pollen which, in turn, create more plants.

All life on this planet depends on chlorophyll. When you eat a lump of beef you can be sure that it was made from green plants in the first place. The ox ate the plants and thus made the beef. Even a plant that is not green, like a mushroom, lives off others that are, or their decaying remains.

So, we must give our plants soil that is sufficiently loose for them to force their roots down into it, but at the same time pressed firm enough against the roots to allow the water and nutrients to get through. We must make sure the plants have enough light (most want direct sunlight but some like shade), and, most important of all, that they are not crowded together with other plants. You wouldn't like it much if you had to share your bed with six other people and have them all trying to grab food off the same plate as you. Plants are the same. So they must have enough room and no weeds. (At the back of the book I describe a new method of gardening called **Deep Bed,** which does enable you to plant things more closely together.)

Remember, weeds are tougher than your plants; they have been bred by nature to survive in the soil. Your plants have been cultivated by people as things to eat, and some of their original toughness has been lost. Which means if you don't help them, the weeds will win.

1.

3.

2.

JONATHON·COUDRILLE

4.

Preparing the Ground

Now what do you do if you manage to get hold of a piece of garden and want to grow things in it? We will assume that it is ground that has been a garden before; that it's more or less bare earth (probably with some weeds on it), but not turf or thick grass.

Let's say you want to plant some seed. If you just throw the seed on top of the ground the birds will eat it, and that will be that. So you must get it **into** the ground. But the ground will probably be hard and trodden, and there are those weeds. If the weeds are large, you can pull them out and put them on the compost heap. But the other thing you can do (and what most people do) is just bury them.

You dig with a spade. If there aren't too many weeds, you may find it quicker to use a fork. First you dig a trench at one end of your garden, as in the picture. Into this you put the next lot of weeds. Then you dig another trench, throwing the earth from this into the first one. And so you go on until you get to the other end. You will be left, of course, with a ridge of earth at the first end and an unfilled trench at the other. Some people say you ought to use this earth to fill in the open trench. I merely throw it behind me when I start to dig, and it just mixes in and gets lost.

If the ground is level, you should start from the opposite end next time you dig so as to move all the earth the other way. But that doesn't really matter much. (Now read the section on Deep Bed gardening and decide if you want to try out at least one bed using this method before you go any further.)

Having dug the land, you will find it is too lumpy to plant seed in. Most seeds are very small and if one of them ends up underneath a huge clod, the tiny plant that comes from it will die before it reaches the light. So you must break up the ground more. In doing this you must use a lot of something that I hope we have all been born with – Old Mother Common Sense.

Supposing your land is very heavy – that it has a lot of clay in it – and it has been raining recently. You try to break up the clods and find it's rather like raking Christmas pudding. So what do you do? You leave it until it dries out, then rake it.

But suppose it's heavy clay and very dry, and has set like concrete. You rake and rake but the clods just won't fall apart. Well, you wait until it rains a little and softens them up, and then you do it.

If it is light land (plenty of sand in it), it is much easier to break up. You can rake it very soon after rain, and you don't have to do it too much either. Sandy soil is easier to work, easier to drain (in fact you probably won't have to drain it at all), and it grows crops earlier. But, like all soil, it needs feeding.

Feeding the Soil

We have seen that plants need food. If you keep growing plants on a piece of soil and taking them out without ever putting anything back, that soil will grow less and less crops until it hardly produces any at all. So we must put something back into the land.

The chemicals that plants are generally in greatest need of are nitrogen, phosphorous, potash and lime. Some people will tell you that if you buy these from a shop every year and put them on the land, you will get bumper crops.

But there are serious disadvantages to doing this. Firstly, the use of such chemicals (excepting lime in certain circumstances) does no permanent good to the soil. It merely feeds that year's crop and is washed away before the next year. This is because you are feeding the **crop** and not the **soil.** Secondly, if you keep putting chemicals on the soil you will kill all the life that's in it.

Good soil is full of living things. Billions of bacteria, fungi or mould organisms, worms, beetles, living creatures of all sorts. These things make a balanced life in the soil, keeping each other in check, and contribute to its health and vitality. There are many kinds of **nitrogen-fixing** bacteria, for example. They extract nitrogen from the air and turn it into nitrates that plants can eat. But if you swamp the soil with chemical nitrogen, you will kill these bacteria. This means you won't get the free nitrogen from the air, and will have to keep on paying for it from the shop.

Soil can become too fond of bought nitrogen – it gets so it can't do without it. And chemical nitrogen is expensive. You are trying to produce food cheaply, aren't you? Well, you're not doing that by spending money on chemicals. And if anyone tells you that you can't grow good crops without buying chemicals, tell them to come and have a look at my garden. I've been gardening without them now for over twenty years, and I have marvellous crops.

What can you feed your soil on besides chemicals? The answer is – anything **organic.** And organic simply means something that is alive or has been alive. We have seen how the chlorophyll in plants turns dead material into live, and how bullocks convert live matter into more live matter by eating green plants and turning them into meat. Anything that has once been alive will do good if you dig it into the ground. Those weeds we dug in, for example, will feed the soil. They will be eaten by a million bacteria (we say 'they have rotted away'), which themselves will die and feed the plants with foods they have taken from the dead weeds. Manure, or dung, which is the waste that comes from animals, including us, is the best plant food of all.

Keep a bucket in the kitchen and put everything – animal or vegetable – that has been alive, and would otherwise be wasted, into it. Empty the bucket every day on the compost heap. Go along to your greengrocer from time to time and ask him to give you all the waste vegetable matter he has – outer leaves of cabbage, rotten vegetables or fruit, anything like that. Put that on your compost heap. Do the same with fallen leaves, or nettles that have been pulled up, or grass cuttings from the garden or the roadside. It all helps.

Compost

There is more to a compost heap than just a load of rubbish. Firstly, it needs to have air to make it rot properly. So just to dump a lot of lawn-mowings into a pile, for example, is not good enough. They won't make good compost and will go slimy and stink. What you must do is mix lawn-mowings with larger, less 'dense' plants (but nothing too woody as it will take too long to break down), so that the air can get through it all. Put a layer of sticks on the ground before you start your compost heap to let the air get in underneath. And it is much better if you can confine your heap within 'walls', so as to stop it spreading all over the place. These walls are best made of wood planks, with an inch or so space between each one, again letting in the air.

The bacteria can only break down the vegetable matter quickly if they have enough nitrogen. This they can eventually get from the air, but it takes many months. So, if you can provide them with it, they'll do the job much faster, and better. Any animal manure contains nitrogen. If you keep rabbits or hens or goats, their manure is fine for the compost heap. If you can get nothing like this, then you will have to buy a little. But try and get organic manure with lots of nitrogen in: hen, horse, pig, cow, or blood manure, or fish meal or meat-and-bone meal. Any highly nitrogenous organic manure. Build up a layer of, say, 18 inches of vegetable matter on the sticks at the bottom of your compost heap. Lightly sprinkle some of the manure on top. Then add another layer of vegetable waste. Then another sprinkling of manure; and so on.

A compost heap is like a fire. It burns, but it burns very slowly. It gets quite hot, too; sometimes you can hardly bear your hand in it. When the heap has 'burnt' like this (the 'burning' is caused by the bacteria oxydising the vegetable matter – which is all a fire does), it is a good thing to **turn** it. Make another heap of it, putting the top to the bottom and the outside to the inside. This will aerate it, and it will 'burn' again. Then, after 3 or 4 months, it will be lovely compost – chocolate-brown, crumbly, sweet-smelling – and that's the time to put it on your garden and dig it in.

Some people just leave it on top of the ground and let the worms pull it down for them. But I prefer to dig compost in, because it makes the roots of the plants go **down** in search of it.

JONATHON COUDRILLE

Make sure the air gets in.

Lime

As we learn in Chemistry at school anything can be alkaline or acid. If something is acid it turns litmus paper red; if alkaline, blue. If you put an acid and an alkali together, they neutralize each other.

If soil is very acid it won't grow anything. If it is less acid, it will grow some things but not others. If it is too alkaline (the opposite of acid), it will only grow certain things. If it is just right, it will grow practically anything. (It is most unlikely, unless you live in Western America, that your soil will be too alkaline. If it is, mix plenty of compost in and you will cure it.)

If you go to a garden shop or a large chemist you can buy, quite cheaply, a kit for testing the acidity or alkalinity of your land. The instructions are very simple to follow. If your soil proves to be too acid, buy a bag of lime from the garden shop and sprinkle some on. Lime, which is either ground chalk and limestone, or burnt and slaked chalk and limestone, is a very strong and cheap alkali. It will neutralize the acidity of the soil and make the land 'sweet', as gardeners say.

The bean-and-pea family love alkaline soil most of all, with members of the cabbage tribe running a close second, so it is best to put lime on before planting any of these varieties. But don't put it on before you plant potatoes or celery, because they don't like lime. If your land is not acid, there's no need to use lime at all. Incidentally, the soil-testing kit gives detailed instructions about how much to put on.

This may all sound a little complicated, but don't be put off by it. If you don't want to be bothered the first year or two with making compost or putting on lime, just go ahead and plant anyway. You will get some crops coming up, probably quite good ones. So don't worry. Gardening is for fun – not something more to worry about.

Winter

The fun of gardening is to grow things so that you can pick fresh vegetables all the year and not have to live on frozen food out of a deep freeze; but in very cold climates this may be difficult. In a moderate climate though, you can certainly do it. You can pick Brussels sprouts, winter cauliflower, broccoli, curley kale, Jerusalem artichokes, cabbages and delicious leeks, all winter through and right into the spring; and you can have celery at least up until Christmas. You will have your onions hanging up in strings and your potatoes in store. Parsnips, except in very frosty climates, can be left in the ground until you need them.

You will have plenty of food, and whatever else happens to you, if you have been a good gardener, you won't starve. Now is the time to get hold of a few seed catalogues and to look at all those pictures of enormous vegetables (nothing like the ones we actually see) and think about trying out a new thing or two for next year. That's part of the fun of gardening – always trying something new.

Spring

It is very exciting to be a gardener in the spring. This is the time when you are planting so many seeds and plants, and watching things shoot up out of the ground. Everything seems full of promise after the dead, sleeping winter – the whole world seems to be coming to life again.

In very early spring you can sow parsnip seeds and plant onions, Jerusalem artichokes and shallots. You will be harvesting (if you did your work last year) lots of cabbage-tribe things, like sprouting broccoli, winter cauliflower, cabbages and Savoys. Also leeks – a marvellous stand-by in the late winter and early spring. And you should have plenty of potatoes and onions left in store. So you could be practically feeding the entire family, even at this early time of the year.

In March and April, sowing goes on even faster. Peas are planted in the garden and all the cabbage tribe go into the seed-bed. Sow lettuce and radish out of doors; also carrots, beetroot, spring onions, turnips and broad beans – if you haven't got some good winter ones. And this is the time (traditionally at Easter) to plant your main crop of potatoes.

In May you plant the bean family –

runners, French, dwarf and haricots. You can sow cucumbers under a frame or cloche – or in the open if it's really hot.

Early Summer

In June you can relax with the sowing of seed, but there will be a lot of **planting out** to do.

And you can do some **successional** sowing – that means sowing more of what you have already put in, so you can go on eating the crops longer. Like lettuces, radishes, peas and dwarf beans. If you haven't planted out all your cabbage tribe and leeks, plant them out now. As for eating – which after all is what it's all about – you may be lifting early potatoes in June. And broad beans, early peas, lettuces and other salad stuffs.

There's one thing you must not forget. That is, **hoe.** Hoe and weed. If you don't, the weeds will win the battle they are fighting with your crops – the struggle for survival. In July, there'll be so much to eat. French and runner beans will be coming in, as well as the broad beans which may be now almost at an end. Plenty of new potatoes and peas galore – not those horrible ones you buy in plastic packets that have been dried and made green again, or quick frozen; but fresh, luscious peas.

Late Summer

It's a good idea to sow spring cabbage seed in August. These will grow slowly, sleep through the winter, more or less, then grow quickly in the spring and be ready to eat when there isn't much else. Otherwise there's very little sowing and planting to do. Just weeding and eating – French beans, globe artichokes, and all the salad crops.

Autumn

Autumn is the real time for harvesting and storing your produce. This is when you should be putting away crops to feed on through the long winter months, just like a squirrel. There may still be some runner beans to salt down in a crock; there are onions that you can hang in strings in a cool, airy place (but where no rain can get on them); there are turnips and swedes, and, most important of all, there are potatoes.

HOW TO GROW VEGETABLES & HERBS

MUSTARD

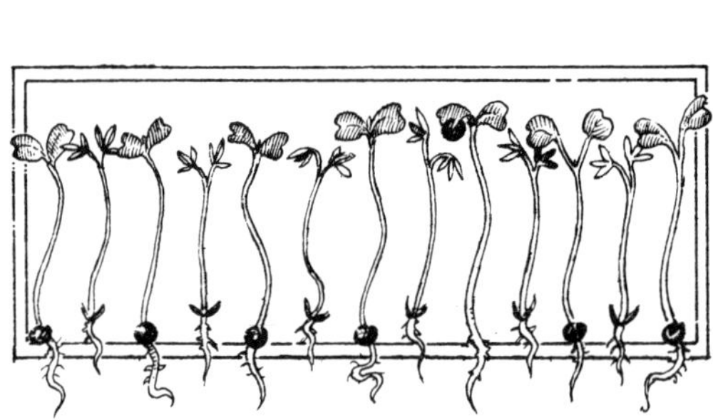

Mustard and cress used to be the one thing we all grew when I was a small boy. Get a seed-box (or any old box will do), put some earth in it and wet it well. Sprinkle on some cress seed and cover with a newspaper. Four days later add a sprinkling of mustard seed (mustard germinates faster than cress). As soon as the plants appear, expose them to the light. Keep the earth moist. Then, when the mustard and cress is a few inches high, cut it with scissors and eat it. It's particularly tasty in sandwiches. You can grow it like this indoors, by a window, all winter.

RADISH

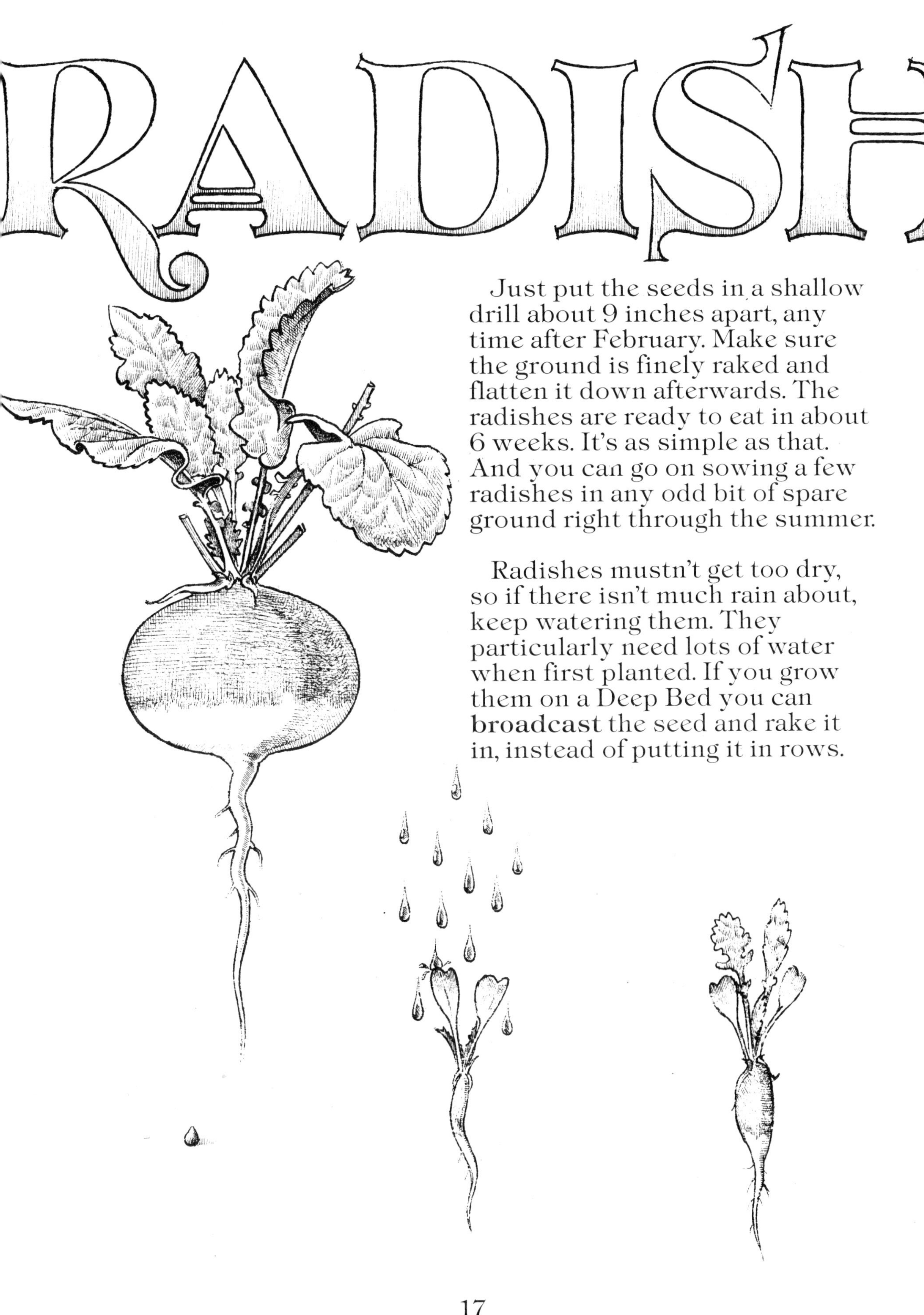

Just put the seeds in a shallow drill about 9 inches apart, any time after February. Make sure the ground is finely raked and flatten it down afterwards. The radishes are ready to eat in about 6 weeks. It's as simple as that. And you can go on sowing a few radishes in any odd bit of spare ground right through the summer.

Radishes mustn't get too dry, so if there isn't much rain about, keep watering them. They particularly need lots of water when first planted. If you grow them on a Deep Bed you can **broadcast** the seed and rake it in, instead of putting it in rows.

TOMATO

Tomatoes can be grown out of doors in fairly mild climates (like the south of England), but they are a chancy crop. In a bad summer they may never ripen and the green fruit has to be made into chutney (if you happen to end up with a lot of soft red ones you can make a tasty tomato sauce). But it's worth trying to grow a few.

If you are a new gardener, my advice is to buy tomato plants from a nursery for the first year. You should have prepared the bed by digging in plenty of compost or manure the winter before (but if you didn't, it isn't the end of the world – do it now, you'll still get tomatoes). By far the best place for the bed is against a south-facing wall. Right up against your house is fine.

Buy your plants at the end of May or the first week in June. You should order them much earlier than this from the nurseryman, so that you're certain of getting some. Take the plants straight home and water them well (give the soil in the pots a good soaking). Then, with a trowel, make holes in the bed the size of the pots – about 18 inches apart. Gently turn each pot upside down, hold your hand over the soil, and shake hard. The plant – with the soil still around its roots – should come out in your hand. Carefully lower the compact shape of soil into the hole, making sure there is no gap around it. If there is, fill it with earth and tap the ground lightly around the plant with your foot. Water well. Stick a bamboo cane in the ground (not through the matted roots of the poor tomato plant though!); as the plant grows, you will need to tie it to the stake to stop it toppling over.

Tomatoes are greedy plants and need to be well watered all their lives – but put the water on the ground, not the plant. A lot of good gardeners use water in which manure has been soaking.

As the plants grow, pick off the side-shoots. When they have got four trusses of flowers on them (the trusses are just bunches of flowers all at one level), break the tops off the plants to stop them getting any higher. If you happen to have more than four trusses take the extra ones off. If you let them grow too many fruit, they won't ripen.

In September, if there are still tomatoes not quite ripe, lay some straw on the ground under the plants. Cut the plants loose from their stakes and spread them out on the straw. Then cover with cloches. This way you'll ripen many of the green ones.

There is a very good way of growing tomatoes in greenhouses or outdoors where you don't have any ground, and that is, the **Tom Bag** – a plastic bag filled with compost, which you buy from the garden shop. You simply rip the top off the bag and plant the tomatoes. If it's outside, put the bag on a path alongside your house or garden shed – but try and make it a south-facing wall. You can rig up a series of supporting stakes for the plants to grow up.

A word about storing. If you put green tomatoes in a dark, cool drawer, each one individually wrapped in tissue paper or clean material of some kind, they may ripen yet.

The tomato is a very good thing to grow indoors. Grow it in a tub or box, or a big enough pot, by a window. Always keep the soil moist, but not too soggy, and feed it well with manure-water, or something like that.

Keep watering . . . and stake well.

TOMATO.

Break off the tops.
Pick off the side shoots.

Lettuce is one of the easiest of things to grow. It likes lots of moisture and a nice rich loam, and it doesn't mind shade.

Lettuces prefer ground that has been well-manured the previous year. But if you make plenty of compost and keep putting it on the garden, they'll grow all right. Dig the soil well and rake it really fine. They don't want firm, trodden ground, as onions do.

In spring or summer just make shallow drills in the ground with the corner of the hoe and sprinkle the seed in very thinly. When the tiny plants come up, thin them (you will have to do this several times), leaving a lettuce about every 10 inches. They'll be the ones you'll eat (if the slugs don't). The ones you pull out can be re-planted in any odd corner of the garden, where they'll continue to grow. Water them in (that is, put some water into the hole) when you plant them, though.

Plant lettuce all spring and summer like this, but only a few at a time – you don't want a glut of them. You can have lettuces coming up in the spring by planting them in August and letting them stand out of doors all winter. Plant winter varieties for this; but you will need to put cloches over them for protection, unless you live in a warm climate. If you're lucky enough to have a greenhouse, you can have lettuces all through the winter months.

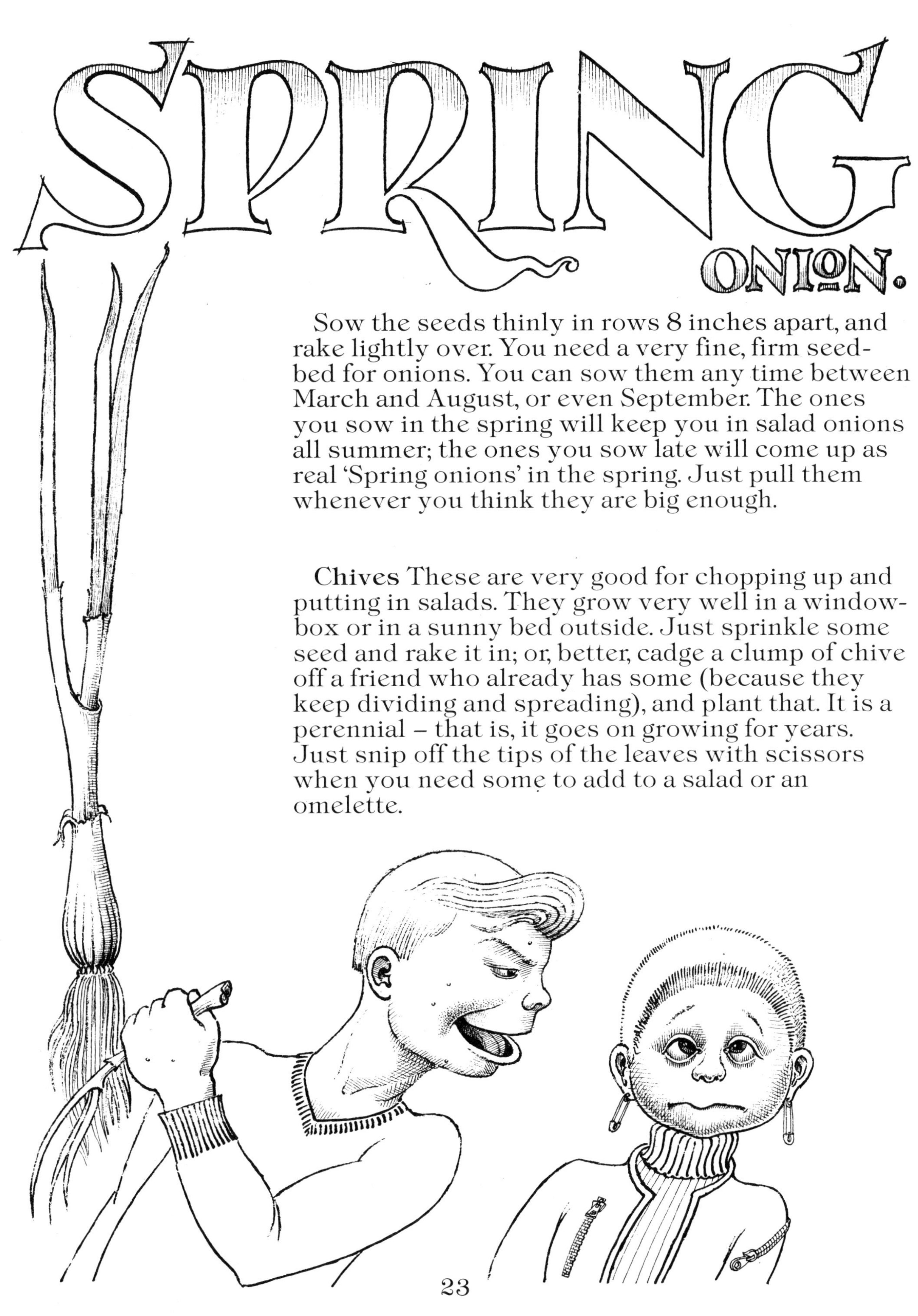

SPRING ONION.

Sow the seeds thinly in rows 8 inches apart, and rake lightly over. You need a very fine, firm seed-bed for onions. You can sow them any time between March and August, or even September. The ones you sow in the spring will keep you in salad onions all summer; the ones you sow late will come up as real 'Spring onions' in the spring. Just pull them whenever you think they are big enough.

Chives These are very good for chopping up and putting in salads. They grow very well in a window-box or in a sunny bed outside. Just sprinkle some seed and rake it in; or, better, cadge a clump of chive off a friend who already has some (because they keep dividing and spreading), and plant that. It is a perennial – that is, it goes on growing for years. Just snip off the tips of the leaves with scissors when you need some to add to a salad or an omelette.

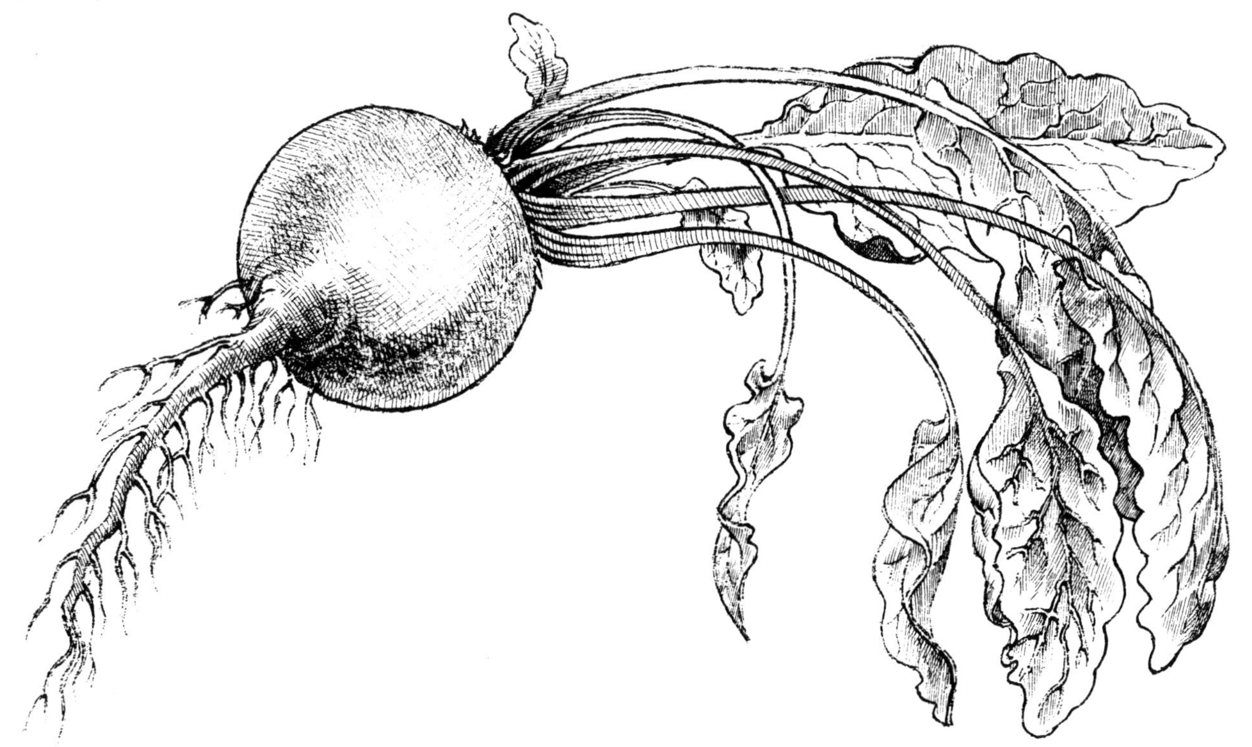

Sow the seed for your main crop in April, but after this you can sow a few in May and more in June for **successional sowing.** The main crop will be for storing for the winter; the later sowings for eating when they are tender and young in the late summer and autumn. When they are quite tiny – no bigger than golf balls – they are delicious. Sow the seed in inch-deep furrows, about 6 inches apart – in rows about 8 inches apart.

Keep them weeded, like everything else. If you see leaves with blisters on pick them off and burn them, for they have beet-fly larvae in them and you don't want these to spread.

To store the ones you are not going to eat fresh, bury them in moist sand in a cool place.

BEETROOT

CUCUMBER

True ones are best grown in heated greenhouses, but you can cultivate **ridge cucumbers** quite well out of doors. Don't grow them on ridges at all, despite the name. Dig a hole about a foot deep in a sunny spot in the garden and fill it up with manure or compost. Then put some of the soil back on top. Sow in late spring or early summer. Plant three seeds, on edge not laying flat, an inch deep and quite near each other. When the plants grow, remove the two weaker ones and just leave the third. If you can, protect the young plants from the cold with cloches or by plates of glass propped up on bricks.

The plants spread as they get larger and take a lot of room. Don't plant too many, and keep them well watered. When it has seven leaves, break off the growing tip of the plant. This makes it put out several branches. Nip off all **male** flowers; these grow on a thin stem. The female flowers have tiny cucumbers under them, so don't take these off. If you don't remove the male flowers they will fertilize the females and make the cucumbers bitter.

When the fruit begins to form, lift it off the ground and put something underneath it. This keeps it clean and prevents the slugs eating it. As soon as cucumbers are ready, pick them – and keep on picking them, so that more will grow.

Keep the cucumbers off the ground.

Protect the young plants under glass.

BER

CARROT

Sow a few in March and then some every month until July, so you get tender, fresh carrots to eat throughout the summer. Just sprinkle the seeds very thinly in shallow drills. Cover them over with a little earth and stamp them down gently with the back of the rake. When they come up, thin them – leaving a plant every 3 or 4 inches. Try and do this on a drizzly day. If you mess about with carrots when it's hot and dry you will attract the carrot fly, which lays its eggs on them so that the maggots eat them before you do. Eat carrots fresh all summer but store the main crop for the winter. Bury them in sand or light earth, in a box or plastic dustbin, and keep in a cool place.

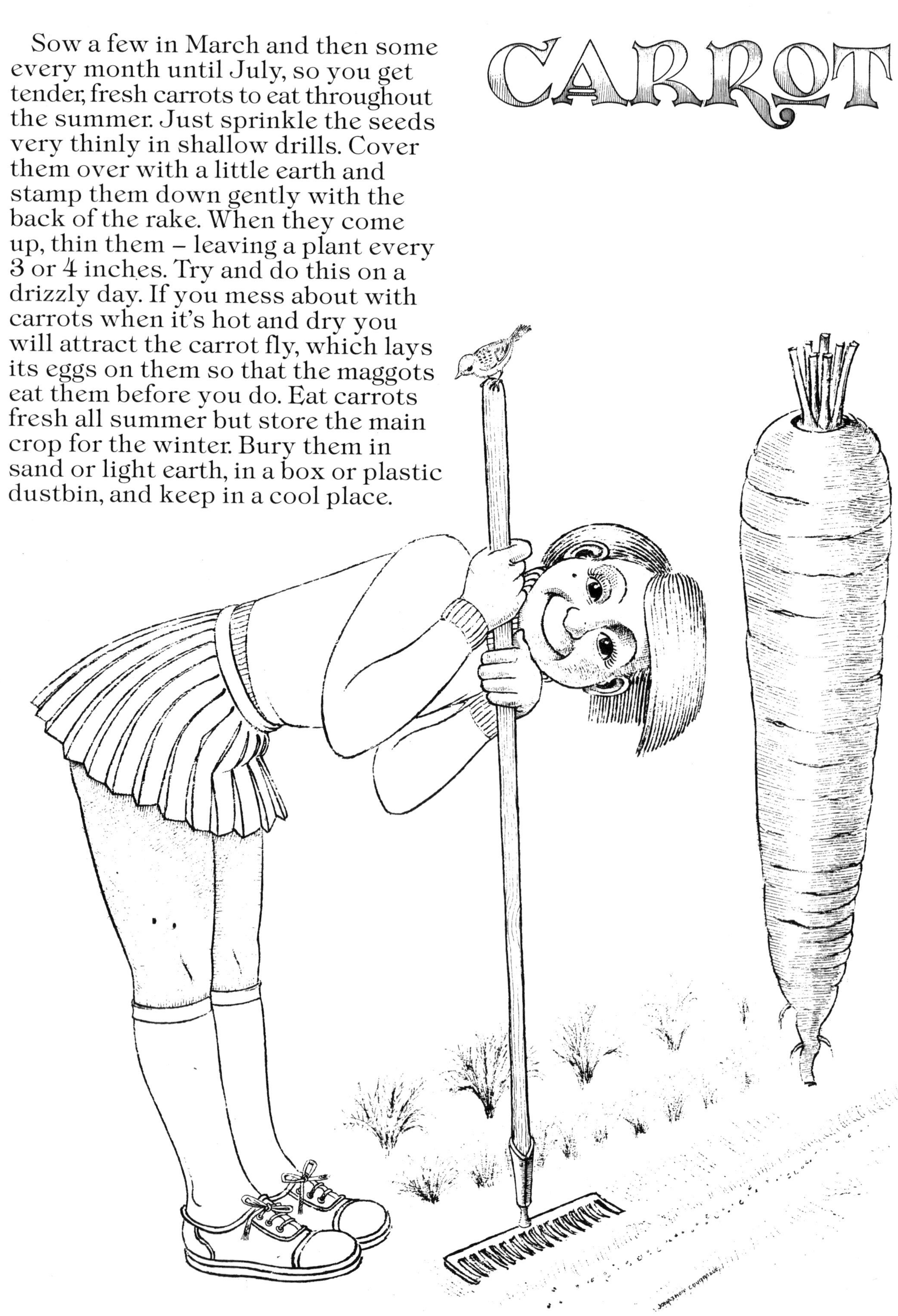

Until you are an experienced gardener it is best to buy young celery plants from a nursery. Growing them from seed, indoors, is quite a skilled job.

Dig a trench, in the winter, about 2 feet deep, and put in the bottom of it 6 inches of compost or good manure. Then put about 4 inches of soil on top of that.

Later, say in May or June, or even July (it will probably be when your nurseryman has plants ready, so you had better book these well in advance), get the plants and put them 6 inches apart in the bottom of the trench; and water. After this, always water them in dry weather; celery must not be allowed to dry out. As the plants get bigger, earth them up – only letting the tops of the leaves stick out. Keep doing this as they grow, until instead of sitting in a trench they are sticking out of a ridge. Pat the sides of the ridge down with the back of your spade.

Eat the celery in the winter, after the first frost; it's a great stand-by all season, if it doesn't get too cold. Very often though, round about January, the frost really gets at it and it goes rotten. You can cover the row with straw to protect the plants, or you can dig them up and plant them in a box with some earth in it, indoors and in the dark. They'll keep for a long time like this.

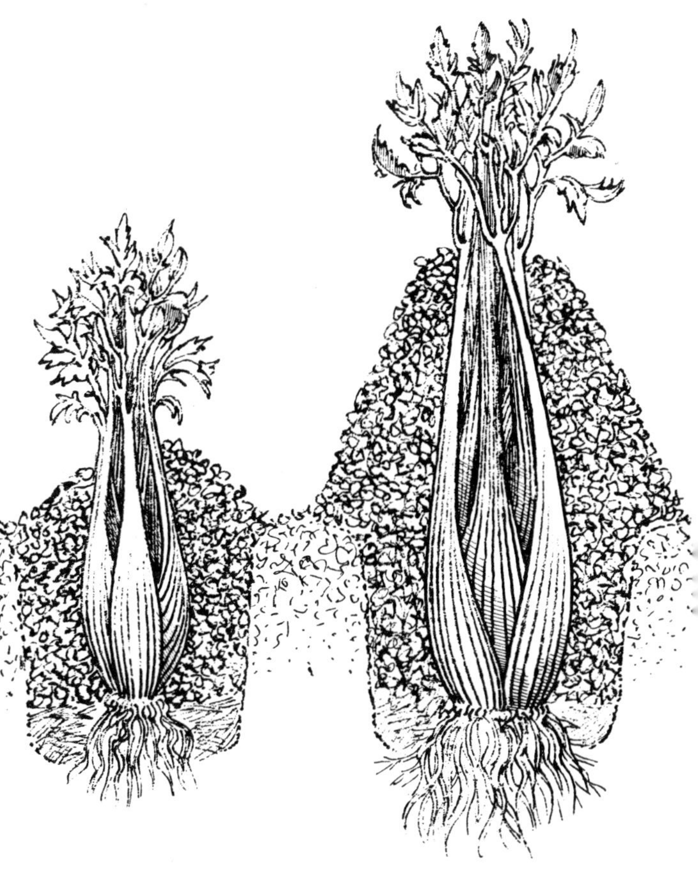

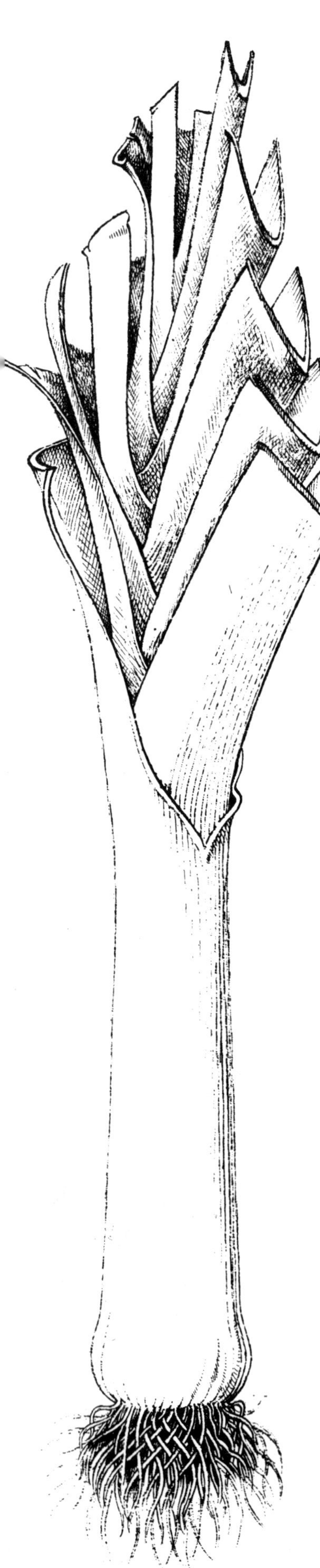

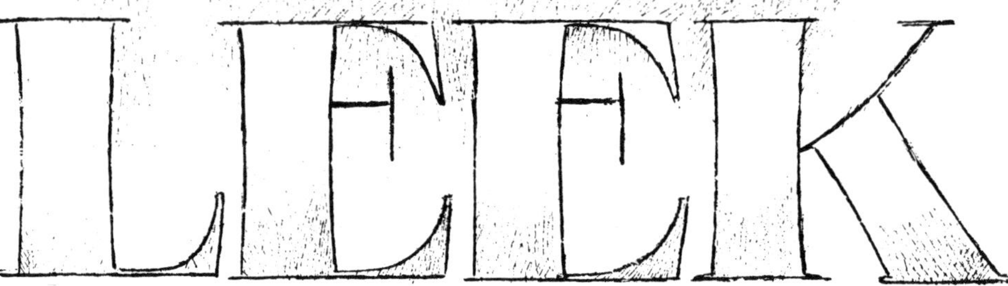

LEEK

Leeks are very easy. Sow them in the same seed-bed as the cabbage tribe in late March or April, and plant them out in little holes, in lines, when they are about 6 inches high. It is best to snip off the tips of the leaves before you plant them. This stops them dragging on the ground and picking up a disease. Also snip off the tips of the root fibres. Pour water into the holes after you have planted them.

Keep the leeks weeded and earth them up as they get bigger – that is, draw the earth up against the stems. This keeps them white and tender.

If you want really huge leeks, plant them in the bottom of a trench and earth them as they grow, like celery.

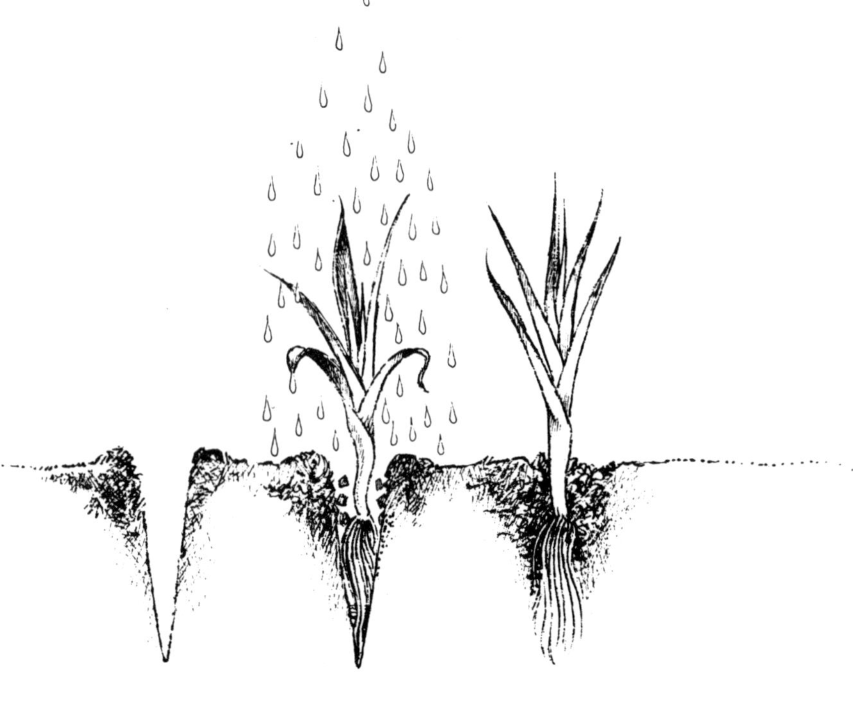

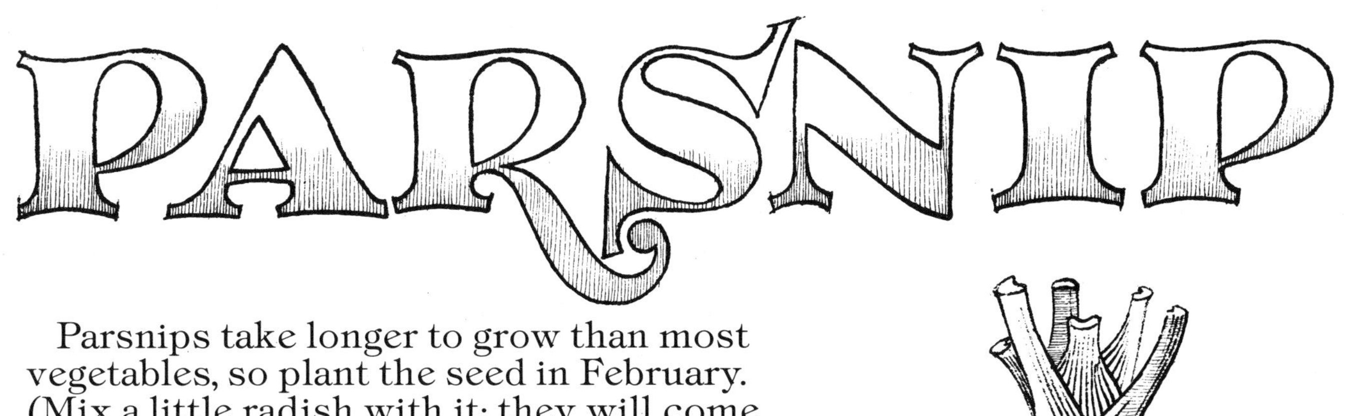

PARSNIP

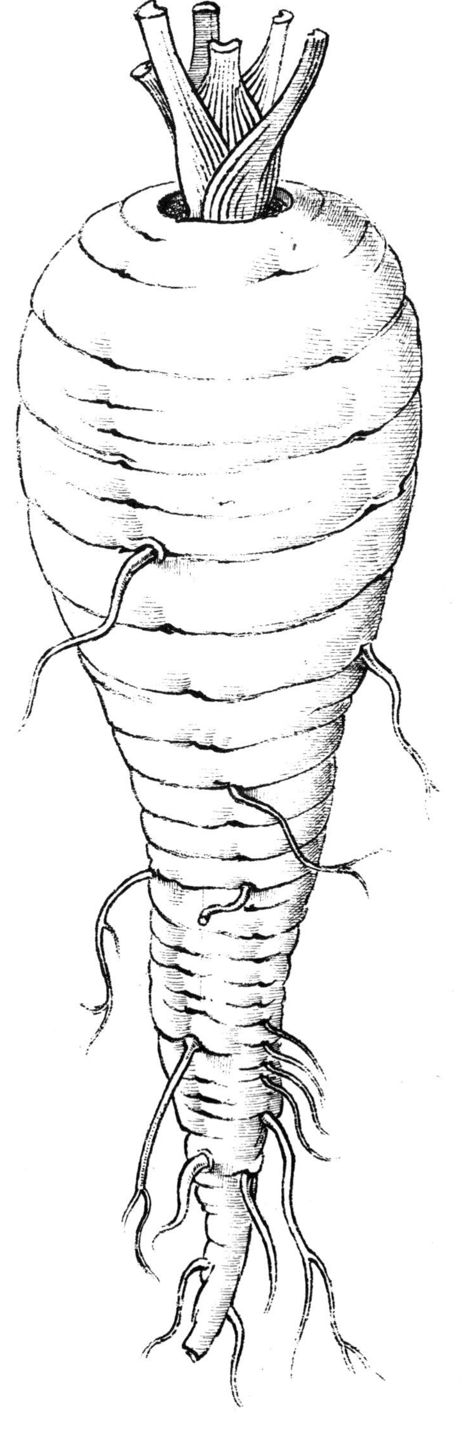

Parsnips take longer to grow than most vegetables, so plant the seed in February. (Mix a little radish with it; they will come up much faster and show you where the rows are, so you can weed alongside them – and you can eat the radishes while you're waiting for the parsnips.) Although everybody says to sow parsnip seed in February, you can leave it till March or even April and still get a good, tender crop.

Sow the seed in drills, about 1 inch deep – three seeds in one spot, or station. Each station should be about 9 inches apart, with the drills 18 inches from each other. When the three seeds in each station come up (if they all do), pull out two of them. In any event, always leave one plant to grow. Then keep the bed well hoed and weeded, and harvest the parsnips any time in the autumn. Frost does not hurt them at all.

TURNIP & SWEDE

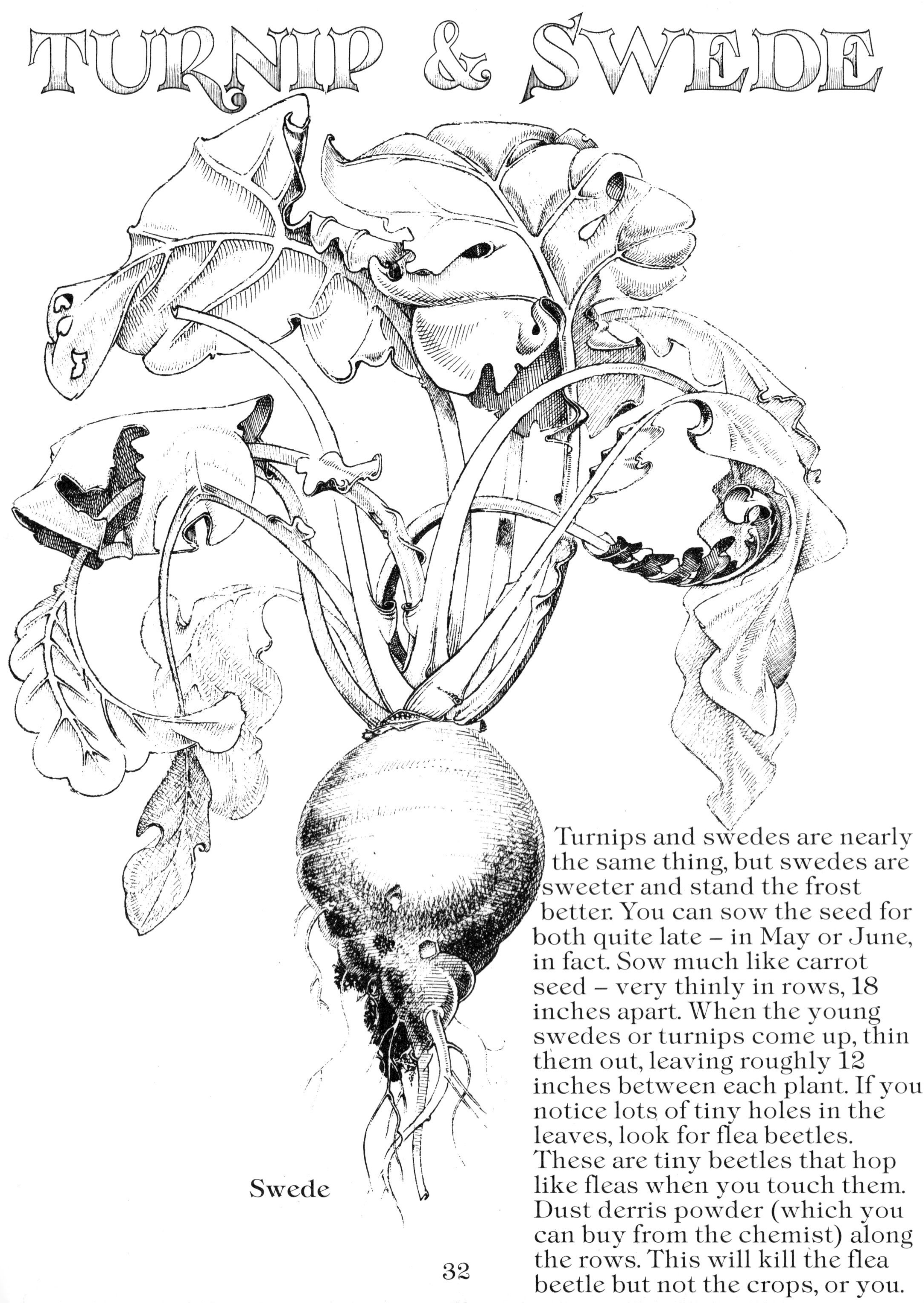

Swede

Turnips and swedes are nearly the same thing, but swedes are sweeter and stand the frost better. You can sow the seed for both quite late – in May or June, in fact. Sow much like carrot seed – very thinly in rows, 18 inches apart. When the young swedes or turnips come up, thin them out, leaving roughly 12 inches between each plant. If you notice lots of tiny holes in the leaves, look for flea beetles. These are tiny beetles that hop like fleas when you touch them. Dust derris powder (which you can buy from the chemist) along the rows. This will kill the flea beetle but not the crops, or you.

ONION

Onions are best grown, until you know quite a lot about gardening, from **sets** (tiny baby onions). Buy these from a shop and plant them in the ground – about 6 inches apart – not too deep but very firmly, in March or April. Keep them well weeded. When they are quite big, bend the tops over sharply; this cuts off the sap and helps the onions to ripen. After you have pulled them, dry them well in the sun for a week or two; then hang them up in strings, or in nets, in a cold, airy place. If you keep onions in the warm they will quickly sprout and go rotten.

When you get more experienced try sowing onion seed in August, in a very fine seed-bed, and transplanting the following March.

If you plant sets or plants in the Deep Bed, put them 2 inches deeper than normal (and of course much closer together – like 5 inches all round).

PEA

Scoop quite a large trench, about 3 inches deep, in the soil with the corner of the hoe and sprinkle peas fairly thickly along it (so that they fall one every 2 inches or so). Then cover them up and firm the soil with the back of the rake. And don't forget, peas like lots of lime. When they begin to grow, it's a good idea to put twiggy sticks in the ground for them to climb up.

If you live in a reasonably warm climate, you might try planting some in November, hoping they will stand the winter and give you very early peas in May. But don't blame me if the frost kills them off. For ordinary sowing start in March, and plant a few rows every month until June. You then get a long season of fresh peas.

If you have more than you need, leave some to dry on the plants and harvest them in the autumn. Pull out the plants and hang them upside down under the roof of a shed. When they are quite dry, **thresh** them (knock the peas out with a stick, or with your fingers). You can use these dried peas for eating (soak for a day and a night in water, then boil) or as seed for next year.

RUNNER BEAN

Runner Beans are great fun to grow. They get higher and higher – climbing up poles or wire or string that you have provided for them – until you wonder if they are ever going to stop. They usually produce a very heavy crop; you can go on picking them for months and the pods will keep growing.

Runner beans want plenty of feeding, though. It is best to dig a trench before you plant them and fill it with compost, and maybe some leaf mould or grass cuttings. Anything that will rot down and make rich feeding, and also conserve the water in the soil. They need lots of watering, too – especially on their leaves and flowers, as this helps them 'set' and turn into beans. But make sure it's a fine spray not a flood.

Sow runners in May – not sooner or the frost might nip them. They don't like frost. **French beans** and **dwarf beans** are much the same, only you don't have to stake them.

RUNNER

Water with fine spray.

Don't forget to give the plant support.

BEAN.

Broad Beans are best sown in the autumn. Plant the large seeds in November – every 10 inches or so, in rows 2 feet apart. Shove them in about 2 inches deep. If you have a hard winter and they are killed off, plant some more in March.

Broad beans want a good, well-dug, deep soil, which has had enough lime in it and preferably plenty of compost. In the spring, if thousands of blackfly settle on the tops of the beans, pick the tops off. I pick mine off anyway, before the blackfly appear, to boil and eat. They're very nice – the bean tops not the blackfly.

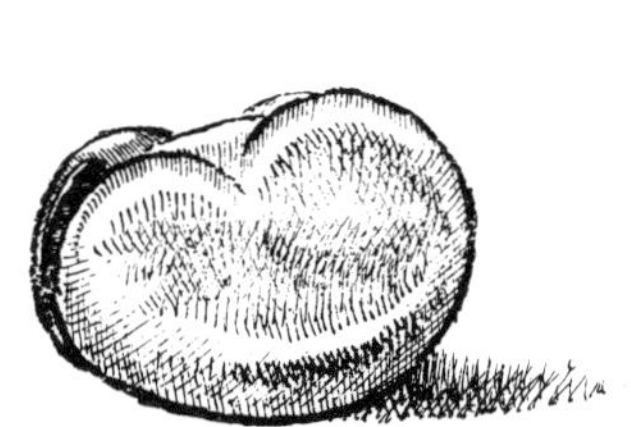

There is summer and winter spinach. You start sowing the seed for the summer variety when the soil warms up in the spring – about ¾ of an inch deep, in well-raked soil. Thin the plants to about one every 4 inches when they are still tiny. That's all you have to do, except pick and eat the stuff about 6-8 weeks later. Winter spinach is grown the same way, but you plant the seed in autumn.

There is also spinach beet, usually called 'perpetual spinach', which is really a kind of beetroot grown only for its leaves. Unlike ordinary spinach, the more you pick it, the more it grows – hence its name. You plant and grow it just like the other varieties. One thing I find with spinach is that it's very bothersome to pick – much quicker to pull out a cabbage than a pound of spinach leaves.

Don't let anybody tell you to eat lots of spinach and be like Popeye, because too much spinach is bad for you. It has oxalic acid in it, and if you ate it every day for too long you would get ill. Just eat spinach occasionally, though, and it's all right.

SPINACH

POTATO

Nothing is easier to grow than potatoes. Just dig a hole in the ground and put a potato in it, and, if it's not too deep, the potato will grow. It will push up leaves into the air and sunshine, and send down roots into the earth. And more potatoes will grow on those roots. After 4 or 5 months, if you dig the plant up you will find the original potato all empty and shrivelled (if you find it at all), but there will be perhaps a dozen new potatoes.

To be on the safe side, though, you should get special seed potatoes from the garden shop to plant and not rely on ordinary ones bought at the greengrocers.

There are some fast-growing varieties called 'early potatoes'. You plant these in March (even put in a few in February, just as a gamble) and with luck you should get lovely new potatoes to eat in June.

The important thing about the potato plant is that it cannot stand frost. This is because it came originally from South America, where they don't have any. So if you go ahead and put your potatoes in early, and a frost comes when the leaves are above ground, the plants will simply be killed right back and will have to start growing again. Instead of having early new potatoes, you will have late ones. The sensible thing to do, therefore, is to protect them from the frost by putting glass **cloches** (little tent-shaped things) or a transparent plastic sheet over them. Then they will survive.

Most potatoes that are grown are 'main crop' potatoes. These you plant quite late, around the middle of April, so that there is little risk of frost. You don't dig them up until about September, and then, if you store them right, they will keep the winter through. There are three things to remember when storing potatoes: keep them from frost (frost will rot them), keep them from getting too warm (warmth will make them sprout), and keep them from the light (light will make them go green and bitter so you can't eat them).

The best way to grow potatoes is simply to make a trench in the ground, about 6 inches deep, drop in the tubers (as the potatoes are called) – 15 inches apart for earlies and 12 inches apart for the main crop – and cover them. If you have several rows, have them 30 inches apart for earlies and 24 inches apart for main crop. But these exact distances don't really matter – potatoes are not mathematicians and don't measure how far they are from their neighbours. Just use common sense. You know how big a plant is; simply make sure that it has enough room to grow. (In a Deep Bed plant them very deep – a foot at least – and each one only 18 inches from its neighbours.)

Before you plant the potato remove all but two of the sprouts or 'eyes', as they are called. Otherwise you'll end up with too many weak offshoots.

As the plants grow, **earth them up.** That is, just chuck some earth up with a spade or hoe so as to form ridges that will protect the potatoes from the light. You don't need to earth up potatoes in a Deep Bed, though.

Try an early plant or two when you can't wait any longer and see if the potatoes are big enough to eat. If they are, fork them out of the ground as you need them. Leave the main crop until all the green tops have rotted away; then dig them up and store them. I store my potatoes by piling them into a big heap out of doors, covering them with straw, and then putting earth over the straw. This keeps them warm enough, cool enough, and away from the light – and it doesn't cost anything.

Plant them 'eyes' up.

Earth up . . .

OTATO

Storing potatoes: keep them away from frost, heat and light.

and earth up again.

CABBAGE TRIBE

Cabbage tribe, or brassica, (by which I mean Brussels sprouts, cauliflower, sprouting broccoli, calabrese, kale, and lots of other things) are the great stand-by of the gardener because they provide fresh green food all winter. You can sow the seed of all these and just leave the plants to grow where they are; but this is not what people generally do. They usually put the seed in a **seed-bed** to begin with; then, when the plants are a few inches high and still close together, they **plant them out** somewhere else in the garden. This way the cabbages, or whatever, don't take up too much room initially, and you can be growing other things. Some people, in fact, transplant them into an in-between place – a **holding-bed** – for a while, before moving the plants on to the final spot when they are quite large.

Rake your seed-bed very fine, in March or April, and make shallow drills in it with the edge of the hoe. Plant the seed very thinly. You can have a short row of several different kinds of cabbage, then one of Brussels sprouts, one of kale, one of calabrese, one of sprouting broccoli, and perhaps one of winter cauliflower **(heading broccoli).** Keep the seed-bed moist if the weather is very dry, beware the wily flea beetle, and plant out your young cabbage-tribe members when they are about 5 inches high.

If you plant any of the cabbage tribe in a Deep Bed, just place them closer together (cabbages a foot apart; Brussels sprouts, broccoli, cauliflower etc., 18 inches apart) and plant much deeper than normal – right down to the lowest leaves.

CABBAGE.

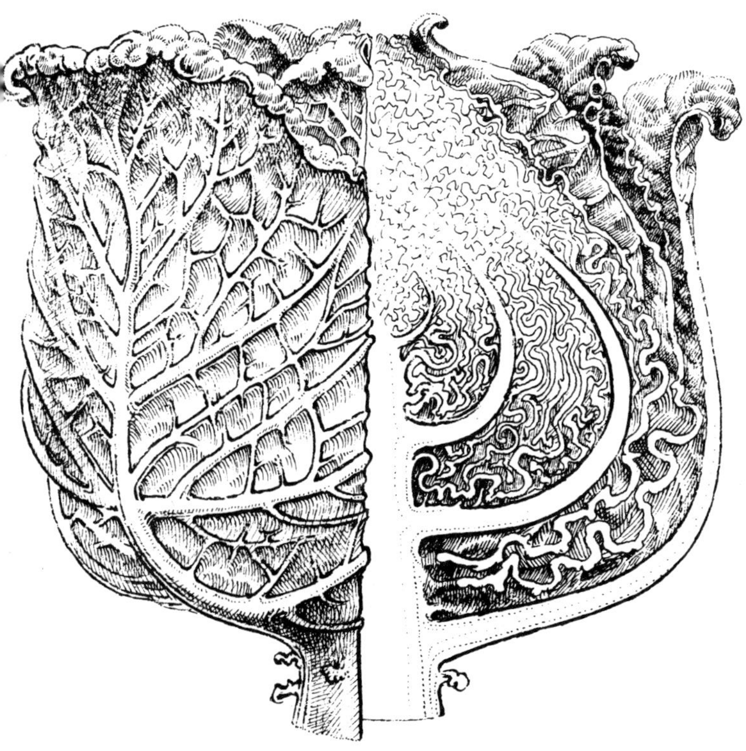

Cabbage, unlike many of the other brassica, doesn't mind recently dug ground that hasn't been tramped quite firm. But it likes rich soil and plenty of lime. If you haven't got room for the young cabbage when they are ready to leave the seed-bed, put them into a holding-bed for a while – 6 inches apart. They will grow quite happily there until you have found a permanent place, and improve by being planted twice.

Sow some winter cabbages in May and plant them out in August – maybe in the area from which you have harvested your beans and peas. They'll grow slowly and give you cabbages in the winter. Savoys are particularly good for this as they are very hardy.

For true spring cabbage, sow the seed in August and transplant them in September. Plant them about a foot apart. If you sowed them straight into their permanent bed, **thin** them to a foot apart. The cabbages will mark time all winter and then grow quickly in the spring (particularly if you feed them with some manure-water), giving you nice fresh greens for springtime and early summer.

Brussels Sprouts Sow the seed in March/April and transplant into a very firm bed when they are 4 to 6 inches high. Plant about every 2 feet, in rows 30 inches apart, so that they have plenty of room. You will then have Brussels sprouts to eat early autumn onwards.

Cauliflower, Sprouting Broccoli, Calabrese Summer or autumn cauliflower is very difficult to grow. Sow the seed in April, and transplant in June or July; never let the ground dry out. The bed you transplant them into must be very rich and firm.

Winter cauliflowers and sprouting broccoli etc. are much easier to grow. Sow the seed in April and transplant into a very firm bed when they are 4 to 6 inches high. They will be ready to eat in late autumn through to the following spring, depending on the variety. Make sure you give them plenty of room when you plant them – 2 feet between each one, in rows about 30 inches apart.

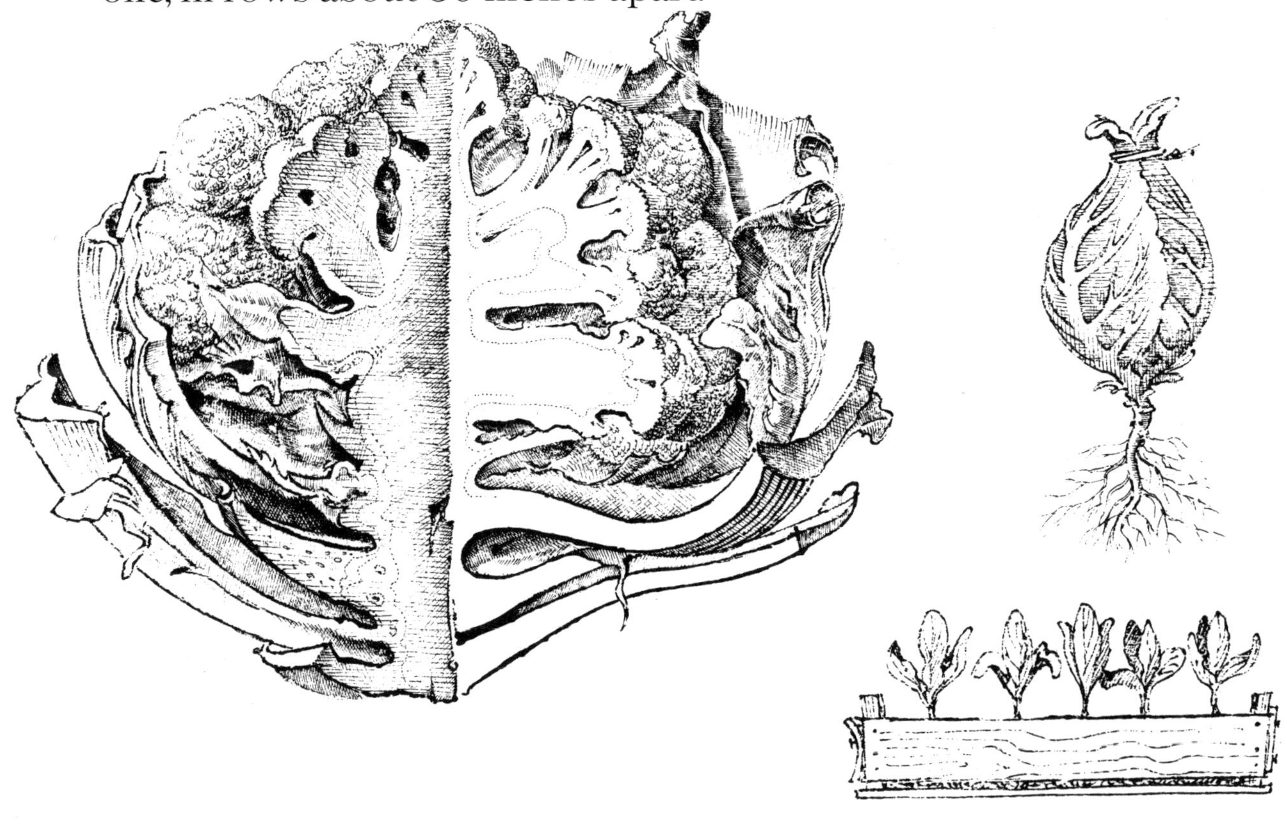

CAULIFLOWER

JERUSALEM ARTICHOKE

These look like rather knobbly potatoes, but taste quite different. You either like them or you don't. They will grow in almost any conditions; in fact, it's harder to **stop** them growing. You just bury the tubers (that is the artichokes themselves) in the

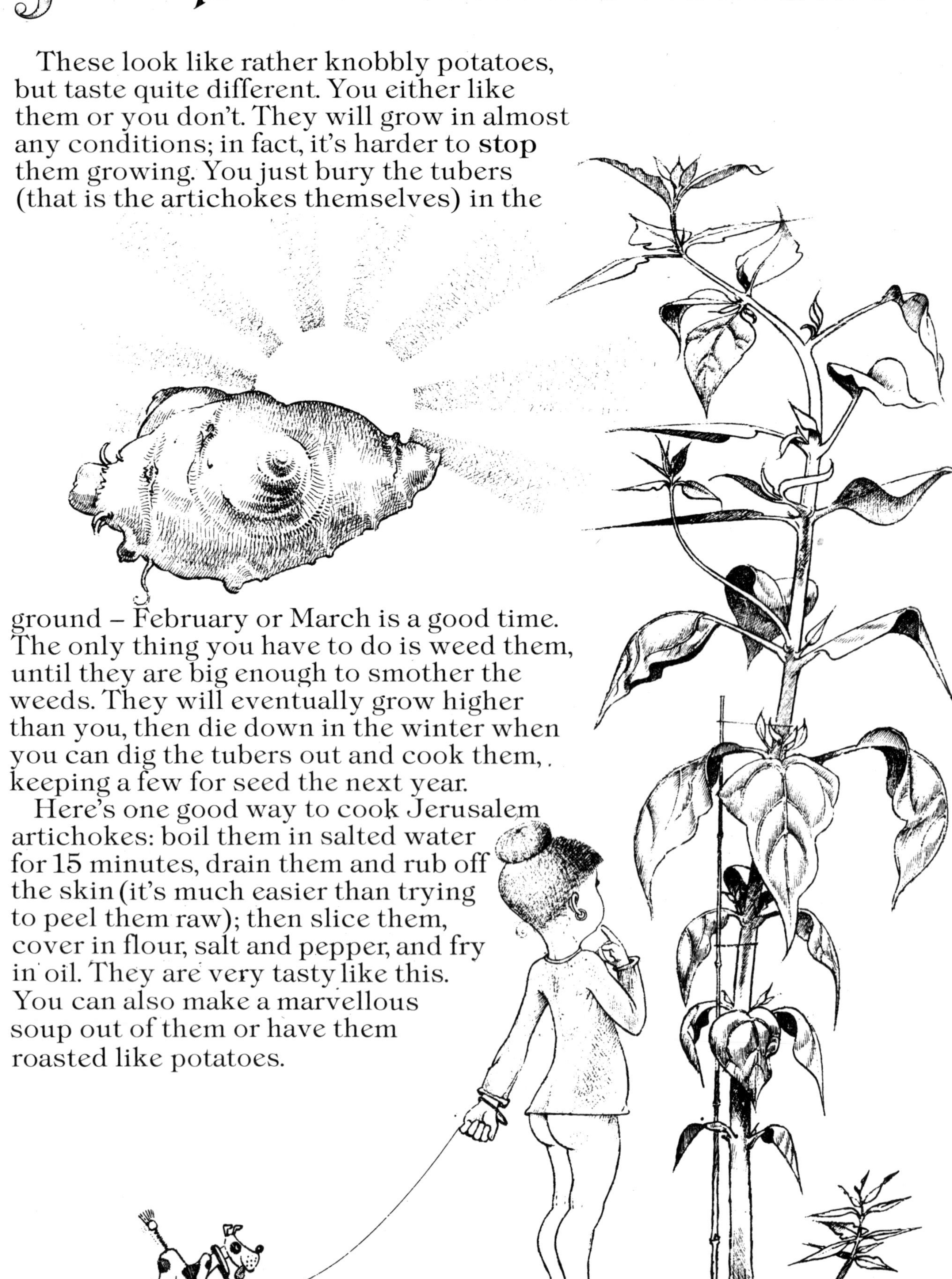

ground – February or March is a good time. The only thing you have to do is weed them, until they are big enough to smother the weeds. They will eventually grow higher than you, then die down in the winter when you can dig the tubers out and cook them, keeping a few for seed the next year.

Here's one good way to cook Jerusalem artichokes: boil them in salted water for 15 minutes, drain them and rub off the skin (it's much easier than trying to peel them raw); then slice them, cover in flour, salt and pepper, and fry in oil. They are very tasty like this. You can also make a marvellous soup out of them or have them roasted like potatoes.

Globe Artichokes grow huge (so don't grow them unless you've got lots of room) and look beautiful. They are, in fact, just enormous thistles, and we eat the flowers.

Scrounge some **offsets** (pieces of root from an old plant) from a friendly neighbour in March or April, and plant them 2 feet apart in a Deep Bed – or else in an ordinary bed which has had plenty of compost or manure dug into it. Plant them so the little growing buds just show through the soil. Water them well the first summer and keep them free of weeds.

Where I live, in Wales, they grow just like weeds, winter and summer (although they do die down a bit in the winter); but if you live in a colder place, cut the dead leaves off in the autumn and cover the roots with a thick layer of straw or old hay, or anything like that, to keep them warm. Give them plenty of manure in spring.

MARROW, SQUASH, PUMPKIN, COURGETTE & ZUCCHINI

It would be quite wrong to say that these are all the same thing, but they are very alike and growing them is much the same. None of them can stand frost, so you must sow the seed after all danger of frost has gone. They are jungle plants so they love moist, rich, humus-filled soil. They grow very quickly and ripen, even if you plant them late, before the first frosts of autumn.

If you just plant the seeds on a muck heap – or a compost heap or heap of farmyard manure – they will grow like mad. But, generally, you can't do this (you probably don't have a muck heap to spare), so plant them in the ground in a warm sunny place. But dig plenty of compost or manure into the ground before you do. Sow the seeds about 1 inch deep, out of doors in May; or better, in a colder climate like Britain's, sow them in peat pots indoors, by a sunny window, in April.

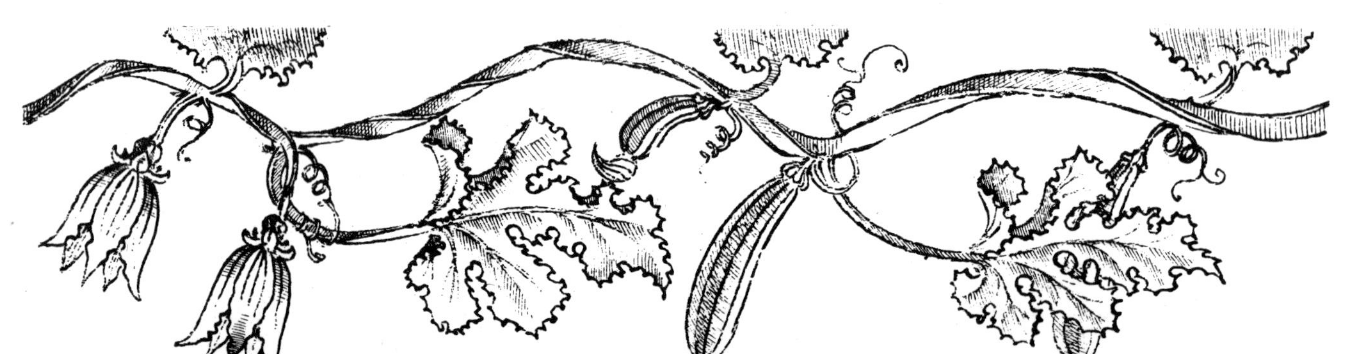

Courgette

When the plants have started to grow – say in about early June – plant the peat pots very carefully in the places you have got ready for them out of doors. But be sure not to disturb the roots – they don't like it. Hence the peat pots.

You can buy peat pots at the garden shop; they are like little flower pots made of peat. Fill them up with nice rich soil, with plenty of compost, and put the seed in. Water them well.

The plants straggle all over the place. If you haven't got much room in your garden, try to get them to grow up a fence. If you twist the vines round and tie them a bit here and there, you can get them to do this. When the vines get to be about 5 or 6 feet long, **pinch them out** – in other words, just break the ends off by a couple of inches. They won't grow any more then.

Harvest all these vegetables before they get too big. Huge marrows are tasteless. Small courgettes (which are really just baby marrows) are delicious. As is so often the case, bigger does not mean better.

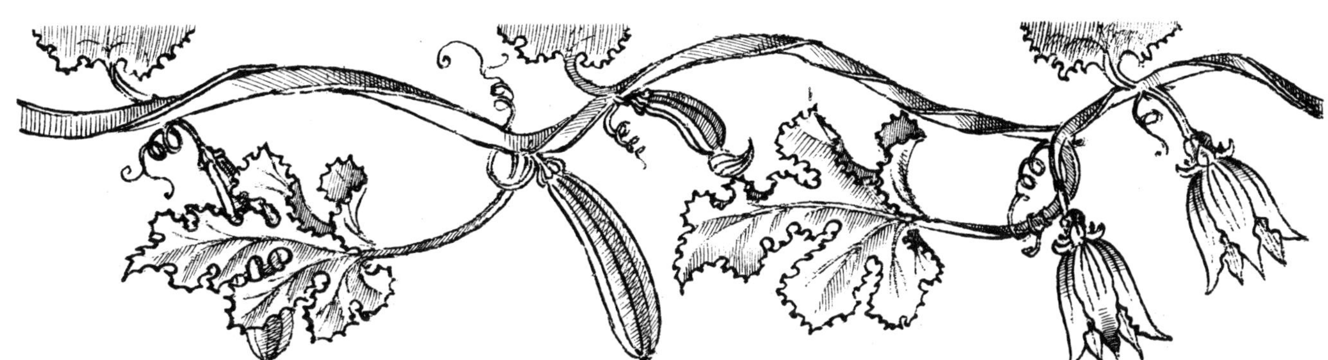

You might wonder what the difference is between herbs and other plants that we eat, like cabbages. Well, there is a difference, as you'll find out if you try to eat, for example, half a pound of boiled sage.

Herbs are essentially for flavouring things: you add them to food you are cooking rather than eat them in their own right, and they make a marvellous difference to the taste. Furthermore, they are full of various vitamins and so are very good for us. They are easy to grow and don't take up much room in the garden. Here are five of the more common ones.

Parsley I said herbs were easy to grow – well, in one way parsley isn't. The reason is that its seed takes an awful long time to germinate (like a month), and if the ground dries out too much during this early period it will die. There is also the danger that other, faster-growing plants, like weeds, will overtake the slow-moving parsley and smother it.

So, in April, make a fine seed-bed and sow the parsley very thinly in little drills, about ½ inch deep. Mix a few radish seeds with it – they will come up much faster and show you where the parsley is growing. You can then carefully weed between the rows without disturbing it. Water well, if the weather is dry, until the parsley comes up. Thin the plants to about 4 inches apart.

If you want a lot of parsley, you can keep sowing it throughout the summer. It also grows well in pots or other containers indoors.

Mint The idea of eating roast lamb without mint sauce is a very bad one. Mint is easy to grow, but beware of it. Once it starts, it is inclined to keep spreading and take over the rest of the garden. It likes a moist, shady area.

Far the easiest way to grow mint is to beg some roots off somebody who has got too much, and just lay them down flat in a small trench. Do this in April or May. The mint will just grow. When it gets too much – after a year or two – dig the whole lot up, separate the plants, give some roots away to somebody else, and plant a few for yourself again.

Sage Another strong-tasting herb. Sow the seed in April and thin the plants that come up to about 18 inches apart, for they grow quite big and bushy. Or you can take cuttings (with a 'heel' of root attached to them) and plant them direct. It goes on growing for years, like mint.

Rosemary Needs a well-sheltered but sunny place, as it doesn't really like cold climates. Buy or beg a young plant or two and put them in about 3 feet apart, as they grow quite large. Do this in May. Rosemary is not very hardy, so it's not as easy to grow as some other herbs.

Thyme You can sow from seed in March/April in a sunny, dry place; or to save bother, you can just pop down to your garden centre and buy a small, bushy plant. After a few years the bush will be very woody and you'll probably have to buy a new one.

Thyme grows to about 12 inches high and has small, strongly-scented leaves.

DEEP BED

There is one very new kind of gardening people should know about (or very old, if you like – it has been practised in China for thousands of years), and that is **Deep Bed Gardening.**

Normally when gardening you dig a bed, break down the clods, rake it fine, and then sow or plant things in rows. The rows may be one or more feet apart, according to the kind of crop. Then you walk between the rows to weed, to hoe, to mulch, to pick off caterpillars, to harvest the crop – and all the time you are treading the soil down flat and hard.

This means that you not only waste the land between the rows (land that you have worked hard to cultivate), but you also make it very difficult for the roots of the plants to go down into the soil and spread out, because your treading makes the ground too hard.

With the Deep Bed method, which has started in America and is spreading fast, you don't do this.

What you do is **double-dig** a fairly narrow strip of ground. An adult might make his strip 5 feet wide; someone much smaller would make it about 3 feet. The point is you must be able to reach into the middle of the bed from the sides without treading on it.

Let me explain 'double-digging'. You take out a trench the depth and width of a spade blade. Then you loosen the soil in the bottom of the trench for another spade's depth by pushing the blade down as far as it will go and waggling it about (but don't bring the subsoil to the surface). You then dig another trench immediately alongside, putting the soil into the first one. Again you loosen it up at the bottom. Then you dig a third trench, dumping the soil from that into the second one; and so on, until you reach the end of the bed. Finally, if you want to be really tidy, you collect up the earth you took out of the first trench and use it to fill the last one.

Very importantly, before you start, throw plenty of compost or manure on top of the ground. When you dig, this will get mixed in with the soil.

Now so far you have done nothing that ordinary gardeners don't do when double-digging. The difference with the new method comes in the planting. When you sow your seed or transplant your plants, you position them twice or three times as close together as normal. And you do it without standing or getting on the bed.

I have seen Deep Bed gardeners in America lay a wide piece of board on a bed and squat on it, cross-legged, when planting. Others just reach in from the outside without kneeling on the bed. This way the earth doesn't get pressed down hard and the plants can easily send their roots deep, or spread them out; they don't have to waste energy forcing them through stubborn soil. Which is why you can plant so much closer together: the roots can get what they want for the plant to grow without having to compete with the plant next door.

If you have several beds side by side, leave a narrow path between each two to walk on, or for wheelbarrows; and that path never gets dug again. You might say that these paths are wasted ground; but, remember, the land between each row is wasted in ordinary methods of gardening!

You dig the bed over once a year with a fork, just a fork's depth. Once every three or four years you may feel like double-digging again, but many people don't bother.

The aim of the Deep Bed method is to plant so close together that, when the crops are fully grown, the tips of their leaves shall be just meeting – all round. One effect of this close planting is that the crop smothers the weeds; it also creates a 'mini-climate' on the bed – the wind doesn't get in, nor does the sun, to dry the earth. So the crops need much less water – about half of what is normally used.

Try one Deep Bed just to see how it works. But don't make it too long or it will take ages to walk round it. Because, as I've said, you must never walk on the bed, even to get to the other side. Except, of course, when you dig it – but that's only once a year.

What about those crops like Brussels sprouts and onions that I advised you to put in hard, well-trodden ground?

Well, plant them a little deeper than you would normally in the soft, puffy soil of the Deep Bed, firm them in with your fists, and water immediately. And you will find that they will grow marvellously. People in America using the Deep Bed method are getting four times the crop they got with conventional gardening. And a better quality crop at that. So it's well worth giving it a go.

TOOLS

Don't let any super-salesman sell you a lot of complicated equipment. You can grow plenty of good food with just these few basic tools:

Spade This is particularly handy for digging ground that has a lot of turf or grass on it, or for very light ground that would crumble and fall through the prongs of a fork.

Fork Most digging goes faster and better with a fork than with a spade. You also need it for 'lifting' potatoes and other root crops.

Rake Get a small, strong, steel one. It's for raking soil fine to make a seed-bed. You can't really do without it.

Hoe Lots of amateur gardeners, particularly lady ones, will tell you to buy a 'Dutch' or push hoe. Well, you can if you like, but you will notice that professionals who have to garden for a living use the 'English' or draw hoe. This is because it's much quicker and does a more thorough job. So that's what I recommend you get.

Trowel You will need this for planting things out.

Watering can Unless you can get spray from the hose all over your garden. But, remember, many good gardeners never water anything at all and still get very good crops. If you use plenty of compost, muck, and other humus-forming material, you won't need much water.

✱Don't disturb your soil in wet weather, and don't walk on it. This is particularly important with heavy clay soils but applies to all other soils as well.

✱Clean and oil your tools before you put them away, and don't leave them out of doors when not in use. Tool handles are expensive and will last years if kept under cover, but not long at all if left out all the time. Oil wooden handles with linseed oil once a year. A good way to store tools is to have a box full of sand soaked in old sump oil. Keep this in the shed and just plunge tools into it when you bring them in. This will clean, oil and polish them. But scrape most of the dirt off first.

✱Keep all young plants growing well. Don't let them dry out too much in dry weather – give them a good soaking with the hose or watering can. Water thoroughly though, or not at all. Light sprinkling makes their roots stay near the top of the ground; a heavy soaking goes right through and draws the roots down. The deeper the roots go, the better the plants will grow later.

✱Neglect no opportunity to get compost material. Does your neighbour mow his lawn and dump the grass cuttings in a corner, or throw them away? Ask him if you can have them; you have got more sense than he has and know they are worth gold. Put them on your compost heap or use them as a mulch between plants. Remember, everything that has lived can live again – in the form of fine vegetables – if you put it on your compost heap.

✱When you go to the seaside bring back a sack of seaweed. It is full of all sorts of useful minerals and elements and will build up the fertility of your garden if you put it on the compost heap. Mud from a pond or ditch is good, too. So is waterweed.

✱Cut twigs in your local park or wood to use as pea sticks and runner bean poles. But do it in the winter. If you wait until spring they will be covered with leaves and not as good – the leaves will shade the peas and beans.

✱Don't, if you can help it, grow the same crop on the same ground two years running. Follow one crop by another, all round the garden. This is because each kind of plant takes something different out of the soil, and puts something different back. Also, the pests and diseases that attack one type of plant usually leave the others alone; so by changing the crop every year you have a better chance of defeating the enemy.

Metric Conversion Table

¼ inch	=	6.35 mm
½ inch	=	12.7 mm
1 inch	=	25.4 mm
6 inches	=	0.152 m
12 inches (1 foot)	=	0.305 m
3 feet (1 yard)	=	0.914 m

Annual	A plant that grows from seed, flowers, makes fruit and seed, and dies, all in one year. Like a lettuce.
Biennial	A plant that takes two years over the job. Normally such plants produce a big bulb, or swollen stem or root, in the first year, lie dormant (sleeping) all winter, and then shoot away quickly the next year to fruit and seed. We cunning people generally harvest them after their first year's growth and eat the bulb or root. Onions are like this, so are turnips.
Broadcast	Throw seed indiscriminately about the ground, as opposed to sowing it along lines or rows.
Cloche	Used to be a bell-shaped, glass hat to go over plants and keep them warm – hence the name, which means "bell" in French. Now can mean a small glass tent or, more and more, a small tunnel of transparent plastic.
Compost	Organic matter that has been put into a heap or pit and allowed to rot. It turns into humus.
Crop	Anything we grow to eat or to use.
Deep Bed	A bed that has been double-dug and thereafter never trodden on.
Fertilizer	Anything at all we put on the soil to feed the plants.
Harvest	To gather a crop to eat or to store.
Humus	The remains of rotted organic matter.
Loam	A medium soil between clay and sand. The best soil for gardening.
Manure	The droppings of animals (including us) allowed to rot down with straw or other vegetable matter.

Mulch	A covering of something put on top of the soil to shade it, keep the the moisture in and stop weeds growing. Any kind of dead vegetation is good, including sawdust (although don't dig this in until it has completely rotted) and leaf mould. Some people even use old newspapers!
Organic Matter	Anything that is alive or has once lived.
Pelleted seeds	Very small seeds wrapped in clay soil, which makes them easier to handle and to sow – and saves thinning out later on.
Perennial	A plant that just keeps growing, year after year. Like an oak tree, for example.
Propagate	To grow seeds under more intensive conditions – usually under glass or in a greenhouse. It is faster and more reliable than just sticking the seed in the ground.
Seed Bed	A piece of ground that has been dug carefully and raked down fine so that small seeds can grow easily in it.
Sow	Put seed in the ground.
Spit	A piece of soil or a hole in the ground, as deep and wide as a spade blade.
Thin	Taking some plants out when they are too close together.
Transplant or Plant out	Dig a plant gently out of one piece of ground and plant it carefully in another.
Weed	Any plant that is growing where we don't want it.

When you go into the garden shop or nursery to buy your seeds, you'll find that there is an enormous number of varieties to choose from. It can be a bit overwhelming. So I've listed the ones that I think are the best. After a while you'll have your own favourites, which may be different, but these will get you off to a good start.

Artichoke (Globe)
Purple or **Green Globe**.

Artichoke (Jerusalem)
Whatever you can get – **New White** is popular.

Beetroot
All beetroot tastes much the same – so any would do.

Broad Beans
Two main general varieties are **Windsor** and **Longpod Aquadulce** – for autumn and early winter sowing; **Green Windsor** for spring sowing.

Broccoli
Purple Sprouting (early and late).

Brussels Sprouts
Early: Cambridge No. 1, Peer Gynt (good for small garden).

Late: Cambridge No. 5, Aristocrat.

Cabbage
Spring: Early Durham, Flower of Spring.

Summer: Greyhound, Velocity.

Winter: Christmas Drumhead, January King.

Carrots
Early Nantes (sow late) or **Amsterdam Forcing** – both good in clay, keep well until October.

Cauliflower
All Year Round (small). Autumn sowing under glass. **Snowball** (for Jan/Feb under glass).

Courgette (Baby Marrow)
Green Bark, Tender & True.

Cucumber
Conqueror and **King of the Ridge.**

Leeks
Musselburgh is the best, closely followed by **Lyon Prizetaker.**

Lettuce
Webbs Wonderful, Trocadero, Unrivalled – cabbage-type summer lettuces. **Lobjouts Green** a good 'Cos' lettuce.

Onions (sets or seeds)
Bedfordshire Champion, Ailsa Craig.

Parsnips
Tender & True, Offenham, The Student – all very good.

Peas
Kelvedon Wonder (June), **Pilot** (Feb/March), and **Onwards.** There are many others.

Potatoes
There is a marvellous number of varieties, though you may find some of them difficult to obtain – but it's well worth trying. Here are a few:-

First Earlies: Arran Pilot, Home Guard.

Second Earlies: Dunbar Rover, Orion.

Main Crop: Golden Wonder, Majestic.

Radish
French Breakfast, Scarlet Globe, Cherry Belle – all summer sowing and fast growing.

Runner Beans
Kelvedon Wonder, Streamline (a long pod) – both good early varieties. **Scarlet Emperor** (an excellent late variety – will go on cropping until October).

Spinach (Summer/Winter)
Victoria Improved – and any perpetual variety will do.

Spring Onions
White Lisbon – very good indeed – you need look no further.

Tomatoes
An enormous number of varieties covering almost every shade, shape and size. Here are just a few:-

Red: Ailsa Craig, Alicante, Harbinger, Pixie.

Two golden yellows: Sunrise, and a tiny one called **Yellow Cherry** (the tomatoes are the size of cherries).

Turnips
Golden Ball – reckoned to be the best for late sowing; and **Snowball** – 'early' and quick growing.